BROKEN-DOWN
JALOPIES

AND OTHER SHORT STORIES
(PERSPECTIVE CHANGES EVERYTHING)

PRAISE FOR BROKEN-DOWN JALOPIES AND OTHER SHORT STORIES

"*Broken-Down Jalopies* gives its readers an up-close view of how Sarah Hellmann transformed personal pain into a ministry where she connects — through art and creativity — with the most vulnerable people in society. These are stories of sadness and struggle, but also of wisdom, humor, and joy. With its empathy and insight, this story collection will inspire readers to find grace and beauty in even the most broken-down parts of themselves, others, and the world at large."

— Kim Bill

"Sarah's stories are heartfelt and inspiring. She does a remarkable job of walking you through her stories as if you are witnessing them yourself. Her wisdom and point of view are refreshing. This book brings me joy, and I can't wait to share it with my friends."

— Barb Griffin

"In *Broken-Down Jalopies*, Sarah Hellmann offers up a set of truly moving stories from her colorful life and the lives of those she serves through her art-making ministry. These touching, sometimes-humorous and sometimes-heart-wrenching tales of the human experience demonstrate our universal need for love and acceptance and our shared capacity to heal and be healed. Sarah's life experience is proof that listening, caring, speaking from the heart, and serving others can shift our perspectives to see that life is a gift and that we are all artists … able to find the beauty living within ourselves."

– Dr. Angela Arndt

"Sarah Hellmann's debut book, *Broken-Down Jalopies*, is resounding proof that creative nonfiction is not a forgotten art. How refreshing it is to hear a new voice in this space and to consider new perspectives on life, pain, struggle, beauty, connection and survivorship from an author who is the pure definition of 'silver linings.' Open the pages of this book to see — in raw honesty and beautiful detail — what the human heart is capable of and why a life well-lived requires both faith in the future and nostalgia for the past."

– Kate Colbert

"*Broken-Down Jalopies* is a powerful book — a call to compassionate action for ourselves and to others. Sarah Hellman's stories about working with the most vulnerable among us will inspire in readers a profound introspection and fresh perspective. If you want more humanity, humor and courage in your life, read this book and then give it to your friends."

– Patrice Eby Burke

BROKEN-DOWN JALOPIES

AND OTHER SHORT STORIES
(PERSPECTIVE CHANGES EVERYTHING)

SARAH HELLMANN

The author of *Broken-Down Jalopies*, Sarah Hellmann, PhD, is not a mental health professional and this book is not intended to provide medical advice or psychological treatment. Sarah is an advocate and supporter of people experiencing the challenges of mental illness, addiction and incarceration, and is a professional educator, jail chaplain and artist best known for her generous mission to support and empower men and women who feel they have been let down by life. Sarah's powerful and inspiring stories are derived from her own experiences with mental illness and addiction, and from her interactions with remarkable people who are starting fresh lives and reintegrating into the world after a time away, physically or emotionally. Information provided in this book is not medical advice, but personal opinion.

CONTENT WARNING

Please be advised that *Broken-Down Jalopies* contains stories
about mental illness and addiction, which may be difficult or
deeply personal to some readers. Readers feeling suicidal,
experiencing suicidal ideation or having thoughts of hurting
themselves should call the National Suicide Prevention Hotline
at 1-800-273-TALK (8255) or visit SuicidePreventionLifeline.org.
Readers affected by addiction: know there is help, there is hope.
Treatment options vary, state by state. Treat yourself with love and
compassion by connecting with local resources.

DEDICATION

I dedicate this book to my parents.
Much of who I am today, I owe to them.

And to all the angels flying too close to the ground.

TABLE OF CONTENTS

FOREWORD: PERSPECTIVE DOES CHANGE EVERYTHING

While I was reading Sarah Hellmann's *Broken-Down Jalopies and Other Short Stories: Perspective Changes Everything,* from what is now my bedroom and my home office, two things were going on in my life. One, the number of cases of COVID-19 in New York City, not far from where I live, was doubling by the day. Two, I was in the house, had been in the house for two weeks and counting, while I was also trying to home school my daughter and work remotely as a Dean of Arts, Education, and Humanities at a small liberal arts college. Our campus art gallery had just closed. Our theater had just closed. Our arts faculty were forced to teach performance classes, visual art classes, music ensembles, all online, all at a remove from our students as they found safe places to shelter.

Like many liberal arts colleges, mine had been struggling with enrollment challenges, though we have been luckier than most. I was finding it hard not to get discouraged when justifications for the importance of the arts fell on deaf ears, and yet again I read articles about the changing landscape of higher education. I was sure that the pandemic would only hasten cutbacks to the arts, at my institution and at many others.

And one day, halfway through my first reading of Sarah's book, I saw on social media a video of our dance students — students who had been forced back home, away from friends and professors and the lives they knew — dancing in their kitchens. The video showed one student start the dance, and moved to another who took over where the previous one had left off. One after another, they were alone in their kitchens but seemed to be moving together as a group. And I watched it again and again. I saw the personal details in their kitchens — the clutter, the kitchen islands, the obstacles and the familiar appliances that each had to navigate and make part of their dance. All similar, but all so different, dancing to the same music, seemingly at the same time. I saw what they were doing as a metaphor for what we were all trying to do — to seek connection and create something beautiful in a suddenly fragmented and terrifying world.

That is what art can do. It is not only for the comfortable, or the privileged, or for those who have it all figured out. It is not only for the elite circles of experts who decide what art is worthy of our attention, or for those who have leisure time to appreciate it. It, as Sarah Hellmann so beautifully and honestly captures in the essays collected in this book, is for everyone, including those who struggle with addiction, pain, mental illness, or who feel isolated or alone. Creativity is a human need, not a hobby, and these essays demonstrate that it is in times when we feel we have the least to offer others when art can help us see a path forward.

Sarah and I have never met, but we have much in common. We are both nonfiction writers, we both have a strong connection to the arts, and we both went to Catholic schools as children. We have both struggled with similar mental health issues and the crippling self-doubt that can come with it. In "Red Shutters: Creativity," Sarah tells a story about being banned from the art station for a year in elementary school as punishment and what this did to her. I had faced a similar punishment in school, and it was equally devastating. What I most admire about Sarah's stories is that they all connect to a message we need to hear right now, in a world that is more broken-down than it was before March 2020. They remind us, like those dancers in their kitchens, that no matter how bad things get, there is a light, and a way out, whether it be through forgiveness, service, grace, patience, and connection. There is always a way.

Kirsti Sandy, PhD

Dean of Arts, Education, and Humanities, and Professor of English – Keene State College

Author of *She Lived, and the Other Girls Died: Essays,* Winner of the 2017 Monadnock Essay Collection Prize; and Recipient of the *Northern New England Review*'s 2017 Raven Price for Creative Nonfiction for Her Story, "I Have Come for What Belongs to Me"

LETTER TO THE READER

When I was in my early 20s, I was admitted to the psychiatric hospital. It was late summer, and I went four days without sleeping. On the fifth day, I began hallucinating. The newscasters on Channel 5 were talking to me by name. By the Grace of God, I had the sense to call my mother, who took me to the hospital. It was a dark, lonely, and terrifying time for me. During one of my parent's visits, my dad, wearing his blue work uniform, and with his giant mechanic hands, wrote on a small piece of paper, "TURN YOUR SCARS INTO STARS." He taped it on to the wall next to my bed. I didn't understand what that meant at the time. However, years later, it is evident to me what my father was trying to communicate. That little note taped by my bedside was my first real lesson on perspective.

In 2012, I founded Art for All People, a nonprofit ministry inspired by my own experiences with mental illness and addiction. Throughout my life, I had turned to the arts to work through my pain. Through Art for All People, I now bring art to people affected by incarceration, mental illness, addiction, human trafficking, homelessness, and veterans who have PTSD. I spend my days painting with the broken-hearted. It is an honor and a privilege to walk alongside people in their journey toward healing. My ministry is my attempt to turn my scars into stars.

I have developed a unique perspective through my struggles and the struggles of those I serve. This book includes spiritual, humorous, and childhood stories written through the perspective I hold today. I have framed my life accounts as pieces of a universal story, hoping it will allow you to do the same.

WHO SHOULD READ THIS BOOK?

This book is for anyone who believes that more things in life unite us rather than divide us. If you believe in the goodness of people, you will find stories that illustrate this. If you are weary, you will find ways to identify your blessings and become a happier version of yourself. If you are willing to grow and change your perspective to become more at peace, this book is for you.

I am in the trenches with the population I serve. At the core of my work, I remind people of who they are. I bring out their creative spirit so they can begin to heal themselves. You will read stories of courage, authenticity, and the resilience of the human spirit.

WHY "PERSPECTIVE"?

I have been called for some time to write a book, but I was never quite sure of the topic. Before writing this manuscript, I sat in silence for a long time in my studio. I looked at the world from where I stood. I prayed. I envisioned an empathetic, peaceful, and joyful world. At times, this world feels far away. Other times it feels so very close. It is a matter of perspective.

I hope this book will allow you to gain insight on how to shape your perspective so you can live a happier, peaceful, and prosperous life.

Wayne Dyer, a hero of mine, wrote, "If you change the way you look at things, the things you look at change." Perspective is everything. I like to think of perspective as a pair of eyeglasses through which we see and interpret the world. If our glasses are cloudy, it is impossible to see things clearly. When our glasses are broken, it is difficult to navigate through life, and in turn, we respond to the world negatively. If our glasses are clear, we see in great detail the beauty that surrounds our everyday life. I am not talking about rose-colored glasses; I am talking about clear glasses that can see the world with all its flaws, and still see its magnificence. As humans, we have very little control, but we have control of our perspective. Sometimes we must take a step back and look from a distance to recognize and appreciate the value in our life. If you dare to wipe your glasses clean and look for the good, you will certainly find it — and your world will be colored beautiful.

THE GOD I PRAY TO

In several chapters of this book, you will read about my relationship with God. The God I pray to is big enough to fit into every religion. I was raised Roman Catholic, so my faith foundation is Christian. I write using the pronouns He/Him/His because I identify with a God who is a loving father. I understand that we do not all share the same image of God. I encourage you to replace the pronouns with She/Her/Hers if that applies to you. For those who do not believe in God, perhaps you can imagine a healthy, loving relationship between parent and child.

I believe in Jesus. One of my favorite Bible scholars, Marcus Borg, refers to Jesus' love as "radical inclusion." Jesus loved the marginalized: the women, the poor, the oppressed, and the sick. He believed in the dignity of all humankind. His teachings reached many nations. Mahatma Gandhi, great spiritual leader of the Hindu faith, once said, "Jesus gave humanity the magnificent purpose and the single objective toward which we all ought to aspire. I believe he belongs not solely to Christianity, but to the entire world, to all lands and races." At my core, I believe the love of Jesus is unconditional and surpasses race, ethnicity, social status, and sexual preference. This is the Jesus I know and love.

I have traveled extensively to many foreign lands. I have met people of great faith outside of Christianity. I have visited synagogues, mosques, temples, and shrines. The prayers spoken are just like mine in spirit and intention. We all want protection, healing, and to be loved. Although I call myself Christian, I know in my bones, that we belong to one Loving God who transcends religion. I hope you find your version of God through my writing.

MY JOURNEY

Not too long ago, I was a split second away from committing suicide. I had a plan. Once my husband left for work, I would sit on my front porch in my rocking chair, drink my coffee, and pull my new X-Acto Knife from my art supply bucket. I wanted to slit my wrists in hopes that I would feel something, anything, before I left this world. I wasn't thinking of the damage and heartbreak I would leave behind; I just wanted to die. I held the knife in my right hand and pressed the blade beneath the palm of my left hand. I planned on cutting deep into my flesh.

My Bipolar Disorder consisted of extreme highs (mania) and frightening lows. I didn't mind the highs so much. During these times, I was creative and energetic. Some of my best paintings were made during bouts of mania. However, there are significant downsides to staying manic for too long. I wasn't able to eat. I had racing and intrusive thoughts. I went on shopping sprees, engaged in risky behavior, and made a series of poor decisions. And after mania, the darkness would engulf me. My lows left me numb, apathetic, hopeless, and often suicidal.

I did not walk this journey alone. One summer, in particular, I experienced a long bout of mania. I was living with my parents after returning from teaching overseas. I had been self-medicating with art, alcohol, and cigarettes. At night I would drink a bottle and a half of red wine and paint by candlelight while listening to Norah Jones, James Taylor, and Paul Simon. At most, I slept three hours in the very late mornings. I would wake and begin again painting canvasses all day and night on their back porch. I was filled with creative energy. When my mind was too busy to paint, my mom would walk miles and miles with me. Before my dad left work each day, he called my mom to see if I needed anything. My request rarely changed: a large, blue slushy and a pack of Marlboro Lights.

My dad likens my struggles with addiction and Bipolar Disorder to Willie Nelson's song, "Angel Flying Too Close to the Ground."

> *And I patched up your broken wing and hung around a while*
> *Trying to keep your spirits up and your fever down*
>
> *I knew someday that you would fly away*
> *For love's the greatest healer to be found.*

My parents held on to my broken pieces until I learned how to mend them, a debt I can never repay. Healing the broken pieces required me to admit I was an alcoholic. I was tired of being a prisoner, hiding behind a substance. I went to my first Alcoholics Anonymous (AA) meeting and sobbed without control for an hour straight. When the chairman asked for first-time attendees to raise their hand and state their first name, I could only choke out "Sa…" The man was hard of hearing and a bit grumpy. He barked, "Please speak up!" The women at my table went through all the names that started with an "S." They were patient with me, asking, "Sally? Sabrina? Susan?" They landed on "Sarah," and I nodded yes. The entire table yelled back, "Sarah! Her name is Sarah." I felt a peace and a sense of belonging in that church basement that I have never felt before. The tears I released were cleansing ones. It was a time of surrender for me.

On the day I was to commit suicide, something unexplainable happened. As if it was magnetically drawn, the knife was pulled out of my right hand. It fell on the concrete, and the blade broke into tiny pieces. And at that moment, I felt with great certainty the presence of a generous God. I found my palms open and facing up. Without trying, I prayed for grace upon grace upon grace. I received that grace, and it overwhelmed me. I knew I would live to see another day. I immediately scheduled an appointment to see my psychiatrist and discuss my options. In the following weeks, I underwent Electroconvulsive Therapy (previously known as shock treatments). The therapy was often frightening. I lost my short-term memory. I couldn't tell if I was getting better or worse. There were times when I wanted to stop trying, but then I remembered how that blade broke into pieces. I remembered the gracious God I belonged to. I worked diligently with my doctor to readjust my medicine. And through struggle and tenacity, my medicine changes were successful. In a little over a month, I began flying straight again.

Although I have many years of sobriety under my belt, I still know the struggle. I work toward my recovery each day. I communicate diligently with my doctor to stay as balanced as possible. This book is dedicated to all the angels flying too close to the ground. You can overcome. May you value yourself enough to get help, may you know your worth, and may you find the support and love you need to patch up your broken wings and fly.

STORIES

YOU ARE A ROYAL WARRIOR: REMEMBER WHO YOU ARE

I spend my days in the darkest places in the city — hospitals, safe houses, addiction centers, jails, and homeless shelters. I work with people, including many veterans affected by incarceration, addiction, and mental illness. I also work with survivors of human trafficking, inmates, and the homeless. The people I meet feel scared, alone, and unworthy. I do my best to shine a light into their darkness. Every day I begin my classes with these words:

Let me remind you of who you are in case life has beat it out of you. You are not your mistakes. You are not your addiction. You are not your diagnosis. You are not time spent in prison or jail. You are a child of the Most-High God. You come from a King. There is royal blood running through your veins. You possess the qualities of the King you come from. All of you were born with the wisdom, courage, and strength to rise above the struggle you are in today. Let me remind you who you are — you are a Royal Warrior.

Let no one or no circumstance make you feel "less than."

People cannot hear this message enough. If I am disrupted at the beginning of class and forget to speak these words, my students will say, "Miss Sarah, you have forgotten to remind us of who we are." My heart breaks when they say this because it illustrates just how fragile the world can make us. Words have creative power over our lives and the lives of others. Let us always use our words to uplift and encourage others. Taking a moment to speak simple, kind words to someone may change the trajectory of their life. I have seen it happen time and time again.

Many of you reading this book may not be in the physical dark places mentioned above. That doesn't mean you do not suffer from feeling alone, misunderstood, or unworthy. You may also need to be reminded of who you are. It is possible to change your life and your perspective today simply by remembering who you are. You may not feel it now, but you, too, are a Royal Warrior. Walk in this confidence.

I chose the word "warrior" because, at our core, that is precisely who we are. We are brave; we are strong; we seek to live each day to the fullest; we fight to live a good and clean life; we can choose to serve humanity and make this world a gentler place. And at the end of the day, we leave it all on the field, to do it again tomorrow.

I will never forget the first time I recited Jeremiah 29:11 (NIV) to a group of women at the homeless shelter, "For I know the plans I have for you," declares the Lord, "plans to prosper you and not to harm you, plans to give you hope and a future." Several women did not believe me when I said these promises were found in Scripture. I had to go out to my car and retrieve my Bible to show them it was true. This saddened me on a deep level. I wondered if they felt they were being punished for their choices. I wondered if they believed God had forsaken them. I imagined how very alone they must feel.

I continued to tell the women that God wants good for His Royal Warriors. He has plans to give us hope and a future. We are worthy; we are forgiven; we are redeemed. God can restore our family. He can release us from our addictions, bad habits, and negative feelings of self. We must do our part by accepting responsibility for our actions and allowing God's love to soften our hearts.

I have found that you can't break a person who knows who they are. And this is why I continue to remind people of who they are. You, dear reader, may need to hear this too. When you find your source of strength and happiness in God, nothing can stop you. There are no forces on earth that can stop God's plan for your life. Step forward in faith and pray for direction and perspective. Be still and trust in His goodness.

You are LOVED, FORGIVEN, and HIGHLY FAVORED by your God. God is the Divine Father — a Royal King, and we are His Royal Warriors.

~~~~~~~~~~~~~~~~~~

You are LOVED, FORGIVEN, and HIGHLY FAVORED by your God. God is the Divine Father — a Royal King, and we are His Royal Warriors.

~~~~~~~~~~~~~~~~~~

BROKEN-DOWN JALOPIES: PORTRAITS OF COURTESY

I believe in courtesy — the type of courtesy that promotes civility, tolerance, and acceptance. I am grateful for the times when I have received courtesy; it has taught me how to extend it to others.

I attended private Catholic schools up until college. My high school consisted of mostly middle-class girls. However, my grade school was different, or at least it felt different. It seemed as if everyone was wealthy with perfect shiny families and houses. Whenever there was a chance to be out of uniform, my peers dressed in the current trends while my siblings and I did not. Except for the Christmas Santa brought my brother, Tom, a Coca-Cola® sweatshirt, my siblings and I wore no-name clothing. The girls in my grade wore Keds®, the plain white tennis shoe, branded with a blue rectangle on the back of the heel. My shoes were not the real ones, and it made my younger self feel "less than." During recess one day, my classmate Susan, who wore real Keds®, hid behind the dumpster with me, and using blue ink, drew the iconic rectangle on my generic shoes. To this day, I remember the courtesy she extended and how her efforts made me feel as if I belonged.

I recall another time in the fifth grade when another courtesy saved me from embarrassment. Like many 11-year-olds, my only desire was to fit into the crowd. This was impossible for two reasons. First, I was incredibly tall and skinny. Second, my dear and cherished father loved broken-down jalopies. With bitter sweetness, I remember a maroon 1968 Plymouth he named the "Bat Mobile." My dad drove our family to church in this car. Sections of floorboards were missing, the tailpipes were rusted, and the engine roared. Jesus heard us coming, and so did the entire congregation.

I was a member of the basketball team. From time to time, my archenemy's father would drop me off from games. She wore name-brand clothing, and he drove a new, shiny Mercedes. One particular Sunday, after a tournament, Mr. Archenemy agreed to drive me home. I grew anxious as we approached my street. I knew the Bat Mobile would be parked in our driveway. Suddenly, the new-car smell overwhelmed me. The insides of the Mercedes sparkled, and I felt as if the fancy dashboard was mocking me. Time moved in slow motion. We pulled into our driveway, and there sat the Bat Mobile. Mr. Archenemy casually said, "I love how your dad likes old cars. Isn't it cool?" His words of courtesy put me at ease. That afternoon I became proud of my father's old jalopies.

I recently took a woman named Chrystal, a severe heroin addict, to breakfast to celebrate her three-month anniversary of sobriety. I have known Chrystal at her worst: skin and bones, strung out, spilling hot coffee on herself. And now she sat across from me, with a round face, a sparkle in her eyes, and straight posture. These are the moments that make my efforts real and worthwhile. These are the moments I live for — to see a soul reclaimed.

I enthusiastically instructed Chrystal to order anything she wanted from the menu.

"Anything?" she asked with a smile. She spent ten minutes reading the menu line by line and said, "I think I'll get the soufflé."

I could hardly understand what she was saying because she pronounced it "soff-lee." When I realized the dish she wanted, I replied, "Of course, excellent selection! I will get the same." She was filled with gratitude, the type only felt by people who get a second chance at life.

The waitress brought our soufflés to the table, and Chrystal asked for ketchup.

She said to me, "Miss Sarah, I never had a soff-lee before." I assured her that she would love it. After we said grace, she squirted ketchup all over the entree. I put my napkin in my lap and picked up my knife and fork. Chrystal picked up the entire soufflé and began to eat it like a pizza. I put my knife and fork down, squirted the ketchup, and proceeded to eat mine in the same fashion. It was delicious.

My breakfast with Chrystal reminded me of a story involving Queen Victoria and an African chief. The Queen held a large dinner party to honor the chief with all the British elite in attendance. The dinner was a splendid affair up until the finger bowls were distributed. These bowls were filled with liquid and intended to be used to clean fingers after a meal. The chief was not familiar with this tradition. He picked up the bowl with his two hands, brought it to his mouth, and quickly drank down its contents. The other dinner guests gasped and exchanged whispers. Queen Victoria was an assertive woman and did not want the chief to be embarrassed. She quickly remedied this social faux pas by picking up the bowl and drinking down its contents. Moments later, five hundred guests followed suit.

I love this story because it shows the importance of common courtesy. The Queen saved the chief from humiliation. She also taught a lesson to the British elite.

Unfortunately, it can be human nature to act in ways opposite of courtesy. Susan, Mr. Archenemy, and Queen Victoria all taught me the power of courtesy. They allowed me to feel safe in my own skin, and I am grateful. Two years in a row during high school, my cars were voted worst car on the lot, but it didn't bother me. I am no longer embarrassed my father's broken-down jalopies. I don't wear name-brand clothes, and I love ketchup on my soufflé.

MY UNCLE'S BEAT-UP JEEP: THE GIFT OF GRATITUDE

I cannot think of a more critical influence on perspective than gratitude. Through the heart of thanksgiving, we can recognize our blessings and the everyday magic that surrounds us. Gratitude allows us to stay humble and kind. Every day and everywhere is an opportunity to remain humble and develop perspective.

Not too long ago, my car died. Luckily, my uncle bought a new vehicle and gifted me his old Jeep Cherokee. It wasn't in the best of shape, but as a daughter of an automobile mechanic, I have driven worse. The front seat has a few cigar burns. There is ample heat in the winter, but the air conditioner doesn't work in the summer. The windows can roll down, but not always. Sometimes I forget that the back is smashed in. Often, the rear door flies open, supplies fall onto the street, and they get run over by cars behind me. It guzzles gas.

Some may say this is a lousy car, but I don't think so. A rosary hangs from the rearview mirror. The backseat is full of artwork. Paint is splattered everywhere, and I am inspired by the colors while sitting in traffic. I drive the people I serve to buy shoes, get into rehab, etc.

I allow the women in prostitution to smoke cigarettes in my car as I pray for healing over them. I love that car. It holds beautiful people, prayers, and art. I believe that if I did not operate out of an attitude of gratitude, I would see my uncle's beat-up Jeep as a lemon. Instead, I choose to see it as a blessing.

It can be challenging to see everyday blessings. For many people, talking about their problems is an addiction. I like to encourage people to flip the script and talk about their joy and their gratitude. Shortly before Christmas one year, I asked the inmates I worked with to flip their script. I knew the women were missing their families, and those with children were riddled with guilt. As I spoke with them about gratitude, I thought there was a good chance they thought I was out of my mind to ask them to share what they were grateful for. However, the women embraced my gratitude challenge.

As we sat in a big circle on the ground, the woman next to me said, "I am grateful I have a God to pray to."

"Amen," the group chanted in unison.

The woman next to her declared, "I am grateful I woke up today."

The gratitude continued.

"I am grateful I am six days sober."

"I am grateful there is air going in and out of my lungs."

"I am grateful to be off the streets."

"I am grateful for good memories."

The circle of gratitude was inspiring and left me humbled.

The Law of Attraction teaches us that our life will follow the direction of our thoughts. If all we think about is lack and disappointment, we will attract more despair. However, the more we live in a state of gratitude, the more we will attract the things we are grateful for. They say a thankful heart is a magnet for miracles. Gratitude is also good for mental health. In my experience, when I'm focused on being grateful, it is impossible for me to also be fearful, angry, or anxious. When I have trouble sleeping, I name my blessings. My body relaxes, and my anxiety fades. It works like magic. Our struggle can end when our gratitude begins.

I recently saw the following on a church marquee: "What if all that we woke up with today were the things we were grateful for yesterday?" I think about all that could be lost if this statement were true. There is so much I tend to take for granted: good health, shelter, clothes, food, transportation, relationships, etc.

Years ago, I began a simple gratitude exercise each morning while drinking coffee. On my first cup of coffee, I thank God for all the things I was grateful for the previous day. On my second cup of coffee, I thank God for all that I am thankful for today. Some days it's complicated. I allow my mind to go back into the jail, where I sat in a circle surrounded by women who didn't even have their freedom. I can say with confidence that my outlook on life improves significantly when I think about all that they found to be grateful for.

**If you want to live a happier life, find gratitude.
If you want to attract more blessings
in your life, find gratitude.**

Gratitude allows us to stay in the present moment. Gratitude allows us to fall in love with our lives every day. We must not wait for the big things in life to be grateful. I believe that when God sees how grateful we are for the little things, He blesses us with more significant things. We must start by bringing gratitude into our everyday practice. If you want to live a happier life, find gratitude. If you want to attract more blessings in your life, find gratitude. If you want to be a better version of yourself, find gratitude. Allow your first thought in the morning to be *thank you,* and see where your day takes you.

I WAS RESCUED: THE POWER OF HOPE

There are often no logical reasons to have hope. Perhaps you struggle to provide for your family. Maybe you or a loved one battles a chronic illness. You may love a challenging person who keeps you awake at night. Perhaps you feel stuck and like life is passing you by. Your life circumstances may fill you with worry, anxiety, and stress — emotions that can be paralyzing and leave us exhausted. There is relief in sight.

Have you considered the role hope plays in your life? Hope is not naïve, nor is it a lofty wish for things to come. Hope is an act of will -- a divine virtue. Hope is a living, breathing, game-changer.

I recently began painting with Martin at a home that serves veterans in drug and alcohol recovery. He has an unbridled passion for life and a contagious smile. He requests songs like *Got My Mind Made Up* by Instant Funk. He sings and dances around the room as the others paint. The men like to act annoyed, but deep down, they are grateful for the energy he releases into our space.

Martin was homeless and lived in an abandoned building for four years. He called it his "abandon-minium." He supported his cocaine habit by selling newspapers and retrieving newish items from the dumpster to resell on the streets. His street name was "Hustle Man," and he told me he could sell water to a fish.

Martin was arrested for selling dope. He explains, "I wasn't arrested, I was rescued." He believes if not for his arrest he would have died on the streets. He credits God for rescuing him through incarceration. During Martin's time in jail, he was introduced to AA meetings and other social services. He tells me his hope was restored behind bars.

Shortly after Martin's release, he attended a spiritual retreat offered by a group of Catholic nuns. He was required to write a letter to God. He explained that the very act of communicating directly with God gave him surges of hope throughout his body. He apologized to God for putting drugs before everything else and asked God to restore his relationship with his son. Lastly, he begged God to remove his desire to abuse drugs. As I write today, Martin is still sober, accepting life on life's terms and keeping hope alive in his heart.

There are three elements to hope. First, hope awaits change and fills the soul with anticipation. Second, it requires growth, which fuels our strength and courage. Hope requires active involvement, such as prayer or visualization. Lastly, hope is related to our trust in God and His ability to make our life anew. Scripture tells us, "We have this hope as an anchor for the soul, firm and secure." (Hebrews 6:19 NIV)

You have an advantage over others when you choose hope over fear. When you are anchored to hope, nothing moves you. Storms may come that shake your very being. Noted Australian author, speaker, and founder of The A21 Campaign to fight human trafficking, Christine Caine, once wrote, "Sometimes when you are in a dark place and you think you have been buried alive, but you've actually been planted." We often pray to God to change our situation, but I believe God is using our situation to change us. God loves you today and has a full understanding of your struggles. Don't pull up your anchor, or you will drift into self-pity. When you are anchored to hope, you can't go far because your faith will kick in.

Hope is assertive and meets pain head-on. Instead of dwelling on negative thoughts, give thanks to your God that the answers are on the way. Do you have your anchor down? Are you expectant that you will beat an addiction, illness, or that your family will be restored? Do you expect to be blessed? Hebrews 11:1 (KJV) tells us, "Now faith is the substance of things hoped for, the evidence of things not seen." Although your situation might not make sense to you in earthly terms, trust that you are about to enter a new season of your life -- a season to bloom into a fuller you. God is not limited to earthly things. God would not have allowed it if He wasn't going to use it for your good. Say to yourself, "I may not see a way out of this, but I know God does. I know God can open doors no man can shut." When you are anchored to hope, God will make things happen in your life. Again, I believe hope is a divine virtue. It requires us to trust fully in God's plan over our lives.

May your heart be light and open to receive miracles. Be patient when you are waiting for your new season to begin. Hope will sustain you through trial, tragedy, and suffering. Hang on, and know with great confidence, that God is holding you in the palm of His hand.

You can be an agent of hope to others. Today, I encourage you to speak up when you see something beautiful in someone. I challenge you to be kind to an unkind person; they are the ones who need love the most. Every act of kindness, no matter how small, plants a seed of hope — and hope is one thing our world needs.

A MAN WITH TATTOOS ON HIS FACE: VISIONS OF GRACE

My early days of recovery were insufferable. I was physically ill and emotionally fragile.

It wasn't until my sobriety that I gained a personal understanding of divine grace. It is still somewhat of a mystery to me, as maybe it was designed to be. My early days of recovery were insufferable. I was physically ill and emotionally fragile. Often, I was not confident I could make it through the night without picking up a drink. I knew I had two choices: turn away from God and blame Him for this disease or run toward Him with open arms. I chose the latter. I recall hearing Faith Hill sing "I Surrender All" on a rerun of *Oprah*. My husband put in on a CD, and I listened to it over and over for thirty days straight.

This is my favorite verse:

All to Jesus I surrender
Humbly at His feet I bow
Worldly pleasures all forsaken
Take me Jesus take me now

The notion of surrender was new to me. *Humbly at His feet I bow,*
I imagined myself kneeling at Christ's feet; leaving all my burden
there. And after visualizing this over and over again, I was able
to truly surrender. I felt physically, emotionally, and spiritually
different. Waves of peace filled my spirit and I felt a divine love and
pardon. I felt lighter, more hopeful, and open to miracles. This is
God's amazing grace personified. Grace is a type of love that has
nothing to do with us but everything to do with our God. We are not
our mistakes. Shame will tell us that we are flawed and broken. Grace
tells us there is no need for shame because our weaknesses serve the
purpose of inviting God into our life. Grace assures us that although
we are flawed, we are cherished.

I teach art and spirituality twice a month at a drug and alcohol
recovery center. The residents seem to enjoy it, and I consider it
a high honor to serve them during some of their most difficult days.
One day, I outlined a sea turtle on each canvas. I instructed my group
of 40 to fill in the spaces with any type of color and shape. A man sat
directly in front of me. He was close to 6 feet 5 inches tall, and his
face was weathered and covered with tattoos. Three lightning bolts
were tattooed under his left eye. Some type of script was written
on his forehead and again on his neck, I couldn't make out what
was written.

As I spoke to the group, I noticed how intently the man listened to
me. As I do in every class, I walked around the room to offer encouragement. When I returned to the front of class, I observed the man

with the tattoos on his face. He was hyper-focused on painting his sea turtle. His hands were shaky from withdrawal, but he didn't seem frustrated. I watched him paint and wondered what type of life he had lived. I wondered why he chose to get tattoos on his face. Perhaps the world was cruel to him and they served as battle armor. I saw him as the child he once was before life had hardened him and I was moved to tears. I believe much of society would have judged him as a criminal based on his outward appearance. But for that moment in time, he was so very precious to me. The scene seemed so fragile, and I realized it was grace that allowed this moment to happen. He was open to receiving help and found peace in painting. Grace provides second, third and as many chances as we need. I prayed that God would shower him with grace each day. I prayed the world would be kind to him once he left treatment.

Grace allows us to extend love and kindness toward others when it seems impossible. Consider Reverend Dr. Martin Luther King, Jr. and the role he played in the civil rights movement and race relations in the United States. I often cling to his words, "Darkness cannot drive out darkness; only light can do that. Hate cannot drive out hate; only love can do that." Dr. King's legacy lives on today partly because he saw the humanity of all people. His ability to fight ignorance, bigotry and hate in peaceful protest was a grace he extended to the country.

We all can extend grace toward others. It isn't easy. We must put grace first before all the other emotions, such as anger, judgment, and greed. It means going beyond the impulse to get the upper-hand or revenge on someone who did you wrong. The grace you extend toward another is never in vain. It helps you become a more evolved human being and brings you closer to God.

At times, there seems to be a limited supply of grace in this world. But there is no limit to divine grace. God's grace is very real to me. I have an exercise I practice when I become weak, impatient, or hopeless.

I shut my eyes and take three deep breaths. I open my hands palms-up to collect God's grace, which falls from the heavens like stardust. I receive grace every time, like a gift I feel I haven't earned. There is nothing you can do to make you unworthy of God's grace. It is more significant than our deepest, darkest transgression, and it can remove the shame that too often shackles us.

DRIVING OVER GRASS:
HOLD ONTO YOUR PEACE

Within all of us is perfect peace, and I believe it's given to us by God. There are opportunities throughout all our days where this peace can be taken away from us if we allow it.

Throughout my life, I have worn a cross around my neck. It reminds me of God's love and peace. I have noticed that, subconsciously, when my peace is threatened, I place my hand over the cross and my heart. I do this instinctively as if to keep my peace from leaking outside my body.

One of my favorite stories of holding onto inner peace comes from a life lesson attributed to Mother Teresa. It has been said that one day she visited a local bakery to ask for bread for the starving children in the orphanage. The baker was a short-tempered man and angered by all the people who came to him, begging for free bread. He spat on Mother Teresa's face and refused her. She calmly took out her handkerchief, wiped the spit from her face, and replied, "Okay, that was for me. Now, what about the bread for the orphans?" The baker, surprised and perhaps shamed by perspective, gave her the bread she requested.

In my role as a jail chaplain, I deal with significant life issues. I notify inmates of deaths in their families and counsel them in their darkest times while they are incarcerated. I work inside the big picture. I try not to sweat the small stuff because I have been granted the gift of perspective. I have come to realize that some people operate in the little picture, sweating the small things until they are dehydrated. These are the people who threaten my peace.

When I began my ministry work, I made a deal with Jesus. I told Him that I would go into the darkest places of the city and serve His children under two conditions. First, I asked for His divine protection. Second, He would provide a parking place at each of the locations I serve. At this point in my career, I have been given a parking spot for five straight years. In front of the jail, there is a parking circle. I always find an open spot.

One day the only spot available was in the center area of the circle. The parking space was poorly designed, and the only way to get to the open space was to drive over a five-foot area of grass. I thanked Jesus for the spot, drove my car just slightly over the grass, and parked. I grabbed my badge and headed into the jail. I passed through security and the two heavy doors leading to the elevator. I was on my way to tell a mother that her nineteen-year-old son died by gunshot, and then I would be painting with the women inmates.

I caught the elevator on the ground floor near the kitchen, where male inmates are frequently waxing the floor.

"What are you doing!" I suddenly heard a male voice yell. I didn't think much of it, as I often hear officers yelling at inmates. I looked around and noticed I was the only one in the hall.

"Stop right here! What are you doing?" I heard again and turned around to see an officer stomping toward me.

At that moment, it dawned on me that he was yelling at me.

"I am going to the third floor to paint with the women." I had never met this man but later learned he was a captain.

"You can't park like that!" he barked back at me. At this point, his face was red, and two veins were popping out of his neck.

"Sir, I have not double-parked anyone in and I don't see what the problem is."

"You drove over the grass! We spend a lot of money on landscaping!"

I believed his reaction to me was disproportionate to my infraction and I placed my hand over my heart as I felt my peace being threatened.

"I am sorry, sir. I won't drive over the grass again."

"Move your car immediately!" At this point, a third vein popped out of his neck, and he turned another shade of angry.

I replied, "I will move my car if you like, but if I wait until after my visit, the second shift will have started, and the lot will be empty. If I move my car now, I will have to drive back over the grass."

"Move your car immediately!" he barked back. So, I did.

I entered the hall again near the elevators. The captain was waiting there, shaking his head at me. I recalled the 2 Timothy 1:7 (KJV), "For God hath not given us the spirit of fear, but of power, and love, and of a sound mind."

I looked at him and said, "Sir, for the past six months there has not been a working drinking fountain in cell block G, perhaps the money would be better spent on plumbing than on landscaping." I walked away with my hand over my heart.

Moments later, I arrived at the pod where I would tell a mother the news that would devastate her for a lifetime. As I waited for her to arrive from her cell, I imagined a different world — a world where everyone could see the big picture. People would listen to understand; no one would honk horns leading to road rage; we would recognize each other as brother and sister.

I managed to hold on to my peace. I am grateful I did, as I believe the world needs the best of us. When we choose to give away our peace, we are no longer the best version of ourselves; we are quick to react and are easily offended. We all encounter people and circumstances that threaten our peace daily. Remember that we were born with perfect peace, and it resides in our heart. It is our responsibility to keep it safe and secure. Do not give it away. Hold onto your peace.

RED SHUTTERS: CREATIVITY

I was a very creative child and, at times, it got me into trouble. When I was in kindergarten, my favorite station was the art station with a large easel that held giant sheets of white paper, large paintbrushes, and jars of tempera paint. Next to the art station, sat a large wooden dollhouse with white paneling, roof, and shutters. As I looked at that stark white dollhouse morning after morning, the absence of color made no sense to me.

One day, I did what I thought needed to be done. I dipped my large paintbrush into a jar of lumpy tempera paint, and, with great purpose, walked over to the dollhouse and painted the shutters red. I remember the feeling of pure satisfaction. I alone was able to save the aesthetics of the classroom dollhouse. I was sure my teacher would grant me any sticker I wanted.

Miss Kelly, my teacher, gasped loudly. Much to my surprise, she was not happy and sent me to the office. I would not be getting a sticker that day. I sat in the office, wondering why I was being punished for solving a problem. The principal was kind to me, and, although it would have been entirely acceptable to paddle me, I was spared this barbaric punishment. Miss Kelly delivered a much harsher punishment, though: I was banned from the art station for the remainder of the year! I was devastated. Without art, I didn't know who I was supposed to be at school. I didn't like playing dress-up or tracing numbers. I was lost and confused, and I never took school seriously again.

On my ninth birthday, my aunt gave me a set of 42 colored markers. They were magnificent. I am not sure if I even opened the remainder of my presents. I hid the markers under my shirt for protection as I ran up the stairs toward my bedroom. I couldn't run the risk of my siblings or cousins ruining the fine tips. Once safely in my bedroom, I locked the door and breathed a sigh of relief. I was in Heaven, far away from the party guests and alone with 42 glorious colors. The bed I shared with my younger sister had a white eyelet cover. I laid down and looked at the white-on-white pattern. Without thinking about it, I began filling in the eyelet flower pattern with shades of blue. It wasn't until a half hour or so passed that I thought about the red shutters and wondered if my mother would be angry with me. I don't remember her exact reaction, but I did not get in trouble. Unlike my kindergarten teacher, my mom protected my artistic spirit.

I am blessed to have parents who nurtured and cultivated my creativity beyond the classroom. My mother gave me scraps of wallpaper and fabric from clothes she made. I made puppets, kites, and collages with the remnants. She was patient with me when I made giant messes in her immaculate kitchen.

My father's auto repair shop was across the street from a funeral home. He sometimes brought home huge cardboard casket boxes that my siblings and I used to make space rockets. I wore my brother's big shoes and pretended to be the first woman to walk on the moon.

Creativity is not just practicing the fine arts. Every advancement we know today started with a new idea, and new ideas are inspired by imagination and creativity. Creativity is innovation. It is building space rockets from cardboard casket boxes. Creativity is the invention of the wheel and finding a cure for Polio.

~~~~~~~~~~~~~~~~~~~~~~~~~~~~

Every advancement we know today started with a new idea, and new ideas are inspired by imagination and creativity. Creativity is innovation.

~~~~~~~~~~~~~~~~~~~~~~~~~~~~

There are dangers involved when we are denied opportunities to be creative. The effect it had on me was serious doubt in the education system that lasted until my graduate studies. However, there are much more severe consequences when we do not allow ourselves the room and space to be creative. Acclaimed writer and speaker Brené Brown, PhD, LCSW, asserts that, "Unused creativity is not benign. It metastasizes. It turns into grief, rage, judgment, sorrow, shame." The art-making process is crucial to our overall well-being.

I spend a lot of time in my ministry work, disarming adults before they create art. Sometimes I look out into the crowd and see the "fear of God" expression on people's faces. I try to smile and give them some good and bad news. The good news is that we were all born creative. Pablo Picasso said, "Every child is born an artist. The problem is how to remain an artist once we grow up." The bad news is that life has a way of knocking out our creative spirit. I have found two main reasons people stray from their creativity. First, people receive criticism of their art as children and come to believe they have no artistic ability. There are frequently times during my art-making sessions when people apologize all over themselves, "I can't draw a straight line" or "I can't color between the lines." These are ideas that were pressed upon us as children and are difficult to silence. Second, someone in their close circle is artistically talented and shy away to let it be the other person's "thing."

~~~~~~~~~~~~~~~~~~~~~

It is critical to remember that art and creativity belong to all of us; in fact, we need it more than ever for the advancement of society.

~~~~~~~~~~~~~~~~~~~~~

It is critical to remember that art and creativity belong to all of us; in fact, we need it more than ever for the advancement of society. I am grateful to have been born to parents who valued creativity. And thank goodness I did not allow the Miss Kellys of the world to detour me from creating art. If I had allowed it to stop me, I would not have the opportunity to bring the arts to so many who suffer. I ask you to consider your red shutter experience. Is it stopping you from being your creative self?

A WALK HOME IN ICE SKATES: FINDING FREEDOM THROUGH FORGIVENESS

I have never met a person who has made it through life without being hurt or offended by another human being. This is simply a part of the human condition. Everyone has someone to forgive. I also imagine everyone needs to forgive themselves for inflicting pain, insult, or injury on another. I once heard it said that when a deep injury is done to us, we never recover until we forgive the person who hurt us. Tremendous healing and freedom can be found in forgiving others and ourselves.

When my siblings and I were young, we frequently walked to a nearby pond to ice skate. One unusually cold and snowy day, my cousin Kati joined us. She and I are the same age and have spent a lifetime together getting into trouble. Now, as an adult, I regret that my younger sister Maria was the target of much of our mischief. After skating for a half hour, and when my older brothers were not watching, Kati and I thought it would be a good idea to pack Maria's boots with snow. We finished the deed and ran home laughing all the way. As I sit here today, my heart hurts, knowing my precious little sister had to walk a half-mile home in her ice skates. I made amends a few years ago by creating a painting of an ice skate and presenting it to her on Christmas Day. My sister graciously accepted the peace offering, but the guilt still haunts me from time-to-time.

Packing my little sister's boots with snow is a small example of the type of regret older siblings may feel. Of course, there are many more severe infractions people cause. I am reminded of the inmates and addicts I have counseled over the years. Many have burned all their bridges and lost custody of children due to bad choices. Most of them struggle with forgiving themselves. My experiences as an alcoholic have taught me that unless we can forgive ourselves, we get trapped in old patterns of thinking and return to bad habits and destructive behavior. The consequences of not forgiving ourselves are shame, regret, and fatigue.

As a jail chaplain, I act as a spiritual advisor to the inmates. I will often begin my conversation by asking people to explain their concept of God. Most people believe in a loving, merciful, and forgiving God; yet they can't seem to forgive themselves. Most of the people I counsel are Christian, so I approach the idea of self-forgiveness in a Christian context. I ask the inmates to shut their eyes and imagine standing at the foot of the cross on the day of the crucifixion. Then, I ask them to describe, in detail, what they see.

A woman recently shared with me, "I see Jesus on the cross. His body covered in dust and sweat. Blood is dripping into His eyes from the crown of thorns. The crowd is pointing at him and laughing. People of every age are mocking Him. His knees are bruised and bloody from falling under the weight of the cross. Mary stands next to Him

–– sobbing tears that only a mother can shed. Jesus is gasping for His last breath. I feel like time is standing still."

When the woman opened her eyes, tears spilled down her face, and her hands were trembling. I thanked her for the powerful illustration of her God dying. I reminded her that Jesus loves the prisoners, the prostitutes, and all of us sinners; this is why he chose death on the cross. Through His death we are forgiven, we are redeemed.

"Every time you don't forgive yourself, you are re-crucifying your God." Certainly, we do not know better than Jesus. I hope that none of us will be defined by the worst thing we have ever done." I held her hand and repeated this twice. I've found this approach gets through to people, and they can move forward in their healing process.

The population I serve lives in active addiction or recovery. Everyone has a painful story to tell of past abuse, tragedy, or neglect. I understand why they turned to substances to numb their pain. Just about every week, I speak to a group about forgiveness in hopes that it will inspire them into sobriety.

I begin with Mahatma Gandhi's words, "The weak can never forgive. Forgiveness is the attribute of the strong." Then I recite my speech, "We choose to forgive people who have hurt us not because they asked for forgiveness. People are often unaware of the pain and damage they have caused us. We forgive people not because they deserve it. Rather, we forgive people because we deserve peace. Again, we forgive people because we deserve peace. This is the greatest gift you can give yourself."

When we choose to forgive someone, we take away the power they hold over us. Forgiveness toward others is an act of self-love. The side effects we feel when we don't forgive others are pain, shame, resentment, and anger. These emotions are toxic to our heart and soul. These emotions rob of our ability to be happy and at peace.

Every person deserves peace. Every person deserves to be released from the shackles of guilt, shame, and resentment. Freedom from addiction, emotional suffering, and past mistakes is found in forgiveness. It's a choice; a brave decision on how we can regain control of our life.

Perhaps you have been wounded deeply by another; maybe you, too, filled your sister's boots with snow. Possibly you need to forgive yourself for the things you didn't do, like speaking up when you witnessed an injustice. Whatever the offense, pray that you will have the courage to forgive others and yourself. Author C.S. Lewis once said, "Getting over a painful experience is much like crossing monkey bars. You have to let go at some point in order to move forward." I pray that through forgiveness, you can move forward and be set free from the ties that bind you.

DIFFICULT PEOPLE REQUIRE A DIFFICULT TYPE OF LOVE: LEARNING TO LOVE OUTSIDE THE LINES

I imagine everyone has someone in their life who is difficult to love. Perhaps your loved one struggles with addiction, mental illness, or destructive behavior. We wish they would listen to reason, make quicker progress, and see the light. Sometimes it feels like we take two steps forward and three steps back. We may get frustrated and often feel defeated in our efforts. We need to take measures to protect ourselves yet provide love at the same time. There isn't a rule book. Difficult people require a difficult type of love.

Working with diverse groups of people, with different needs and unique pain, often requires us to, what I call, "love outside the lines." There are frequently times in my ministry work where the lines are blurred when I am uncertain on how to comfort or console a suffering individual. Loving outside the lines can be clumsy.

In these times, I pray, and each time, I receive intuition on how to proceed.

Years ago at the homeless shelter, I worked with a woman named Beverly. During our first few encounters, she arrived late, sat in the corner, and listened to our music. She was visibly drunk, slurred words to the songs, and cursed at people who passed by. One night, I invited Beverly to join us in painting. She abrasively yelled back at me, "I'm drunk!" I matched her volume and replied, "I know! How about you sit down next to me anyway?" She begrudgingly did so. I asked what her favorite color was, and she told me green. I gave her a canvas and made three shades of green on her palette. Beverly began to paint. At first, her brushstrokes were sloppy and clumsy. In time, her strokes became intentional, and her demeanor changed. She was quiet, and there was a stillness about her. I played Bach's "Air on the G String." Her hand danced to the rhythm of the music, and tears fell from her face. I put my hand on her shoulder and smiled at her. She smiled back and said, "Thank you." We didn't speak much after that.

The following week Beverly was waiting for me to arrive. I greeted her, and she said, "I decided not to drink until after we paint." I told her I was proud of her and thanked her for attending class. I made the same three shades of green on her palette and she painted for an hour straight. Her only words were, "Can you play that song again that doesn't have words?" I played Bach and her face softened. Toward the end of class, I asked the other women if any of them attended a 12-step meeting. Many heads in the room nodded yes. I asked Beverly if she would attend a meeting with the other women, and she agreed. I believe the painting opened Beverly's heart enough to let some light in. I am not sure where she is today but I will remember her with a soft face, listening to Bach and painting shades of green.

Early in my ministry work, I met Alex, a young addict. He had no family, no real friends, and he dropped out of high school. He bounced in and out of foster care, where older children abused him. His mother died of an overdose. After hearing about his life, I was not surprised that he turned to drugs for some relief. I wanted to help Alex in any way I could. I attended AA meetings with him and set up sessions with a GED coach to help him earn his high school equivalency. Over time, Alex stopped showing up. He only called when he needed cigarettes and money for "food." His calls became more and more demanding.

I recognized that Alex was zapping my energy, and I grew to resent him. I didn't want to abandon him, so I set boundaries to preserve my peace and regain the strength to continue to help him. I told Alex that I would accept two calls a week from him, I would not give him cash, but I would buy him cigarettes after he accomplished small goals. At first, he was angry with me, but he eventually accepted my rules. He asked what he needed to do to get a pack of cigarettes. I told him he needed to attend three straight days of AA or NA (Narcotics Anonymous) meetings and get the name and number of the group facilitator. He complied. Three packs of cigarettes later, he found a sponsor and began his first journey toward sobriety.

I am sure most of us know someone affected by addiction. Loving an addict is painful and difficult. It is essential to acknowledge their pain. It is equally important to communicate that no matter how deeply they have been hurt, addiction is not the answer. There is help, and there is hope. Behind every addict is a soul waiting to be reclaimed.

When dealing with people who are difficult to love, we must be sure where we stand and what we are willing to tolerate so boundaries can be sustained. I wish it were as easy as setting up a "No Trespassing" sign across our hearts. Loving difficult people is complicated and often heartbreaking. It takes time and practice to find the delicate balance between loving the person and taking care of ourselves. Maintaining healthy boundaries is critical for both parties. Alex knew where I stood and eventually received the help he so desperately needed. The boundary maker benefits as well, by attaining increased levels of emotional energy, patience, self-esteem, and independence.

Beverly and Alex taught me an essential lesson about meeting people where they are. People are where they are, despite our wishes for them to be sober, healthier, closer to God, or simply more pleasant. It is critical to remember that while boundaries are an act of self-care, they can also be a motivator for our loved one to get help. Be sure your boundaries are secure, or you will grow weary very quickly.

~~~~~~~~~~~~~~~~~~~~~~~~

Beverly and Alex taught me an essential lesson about meeting people where they are. People are where they are, despite our wishes for them to be sober, healthier, closer to God, or simply more pleasant.

~~~~~~~~~~~~~~~~~~~~~~~~

Jesus spent a lifetime loving difficult people. Meeting people where they are means giving others what they need, when they need it, and engaging them in a meaningful, nonjudgmental way. It is essential that we listen to each other's stories, hear their plight, and respond to their pain. Jesus meets us in the moment, no matter where we are in life. I try to love as Jesus does. I believe by doing this, we will receive the grace, patience, and fortitude to love difficult people.

A CAR RIDE FROM PRISON: SEEING THE ORDINARY MAGIC

I mentored Brenda for two years while she was in prison. Occasionally, I visited her face-to-face, but our primary way of communicating was through phone calls and emails. Our conversations mainly focused on her college coursework. I would help her with her sociology studies and offer encouragement before exams. It never felt as if I was communicating with an inmate. Brenda reminded me of the many high school and college students I have taught over the years. She had dreams, ambition, and the desire to improve her life.

Brenda had very few friends that were not of her previous lifestyle and no living family except for her grown children. She asked me if I would be willing to pick her up on her release date. When the day came, I arrived 30 minutes early to fill out paperwork and be cleared by security. Surprisingly, I finished in under ten minutes and sat down in the sterile waiting room. The clock on the wall showed 7:10 a.m. Usually when I have 20 minutes to pass, I rely on my phone for entertainment. However, I left my phone in the car because it was forbidden in the facility. Time moved by slowly. I imagined what Brenda might be feeling. I assumed she was happy but scared at the same time. I wondered what her first words outside would be and what our conversations would consist of on our two-hour car ride home.

At exactly 7:30, a loud buzz filled the room. I heard heavy doors open and shut and saw Brenda walking quickly down the hall. She was wearing a giant smile and a grey prison-issued sweat suit. She ran into my arms and held me tight. Happy tears swam down her face. I took one of her clear garbage bags filled with books, and we walked out of the double doors together. It was a late spring day, and the sun was still rising. Brenda took three deep, long breaths, laughed out loud, and exclaimed, "Breathing feels better when you are free." I smiled at her and put my hand on her shoulder.

Time passed quickly and effortlessly on our ride back. Brenda enthusiastically commented on the details found in nature; how the green leaves were beginning to fill the trees, a crow that flew high in the sky, and the scent of freshly cut grass. She rolled the window down and smiled as the breeze touched her cheek. All was right in her world. I tried to recall the last time I felt that type of excitement from observing nature. I was embarrassed and a little ashamed by my lack of memory. As we got closer to the city, I told Brenda we would stop for brunch, shop for clothing at the thrift store, and check her into the homeless shelter. She appeared to look forward to the day ahead.

We stopped for brunch at a quaint café just outside of the city limits. I ordered a spinach quiche with a side of fresh fruit and coffee. Brenda ordered the exact same thing but looked a little distressed as she looked around the room. I wondered if she felt out of place in her grey sweat suit. I wondered if she felt uncomfortable around mainstream society just an hour and a half out of prison.

I asked her how she was doing, and she replied, "I'm good. It's just that I don't know what a quiche is, and I haven't eaten fresh fruit in two years." I explained what a quiche was and reassured her that if she didn't like it, she could order something else. This seemed to satisfy her.

The waitress brought our coffee with cream and sugar. I watched Brenda's eyes light up as she breathed in the freshly ground aroma.

"This is a real treat. All we get in prison is decaf instant and powdered creamer," she exclaimed as she dribbled cream into her cup. "I love watching the cream interact with the black coffee. It's soothing to me."

I smiled as she passed me the cream. I did just as Brenda did. I slowly poured the creamer and noticed how the darkness in my cup turned to swirls of light brown and then to a shade of beige. It was soothing, just like she mentioned. Our food arrived 20 minutes later. With great delight, Brenda first ate her fruit. She carefully selected each piece, chewed it slowly, and savored every bite. I did as Brenda did and noticed how cold and sweet the strawberries tasted. Next, Brenda took a bite out of the quiche. She ate it with the same attention.

When she was finished, I asked her how she liked it. She answered, "I think quiche is my new favorite food." Her love of this new food warmed my heart.

As we drove away from the café, I realized I have never been in the company of someone so content and present as Brenda was in that moment. It made me think of all the crows flying high in the sky that I have failed to notice, all the cream I poured quickly into my coffee, and the countless amounts of fruit I have not savored.

In my relationship with Brenda, I always assumed the teacher's role. On our ride home from prison, Brenda was the wise one. She saw the world with wonderment only children seem to possess. I realized I took so much for granted and am grateful for the lessons Brenda taught me. Since then, flowers smell better, food tastes richer, and the birds sing on key. We are never too old to get our child-like wonderment back. It starts by seeing the ordinary magic that surrounds us all.

EVERYBODY IS A GENIUS: CELEBRATE YOU

When I was in the fifth grade, classes were separated by math scores. At our school, the students named the three groups "the Smart Class, the Medium Smart Class, and the Misfits." In fourth grade, I struggled with long division and fractions. And so, my fate was tied as a member of the Misfit Class until eighth grade. My 11-year-old self was devastated. Up until that point, I considered myself to be smart. I was often selected to pair up and assist the slow readers. My teachers praised my responses in religion class. In gym class, I was chosen in the top three for kickball. Now school looked much different to me.

Frankly, my fellow Misfits weren't so bad. They were highly creative and very funny, but we lived on our own island, where the teachers had less patience with us. Mrs. G, who taught English to all three classes, was the exception. Her clothes were stylish, and her hair was blonde in a bob cut. I remember a few months into school, she informed us that our class was her favorite, and it didn't matter what anyone else said. Her words put us at ease, and we behaved well for her. Mrs. G took the time to compliment us. She recognized my enthusiasm for writing. There were many afternoons when she would privately tutor me at her desk over brown-bag lunches.

We also had a "Picture Lady," a parent volunteer who taught art to the Misfits monthly. I clearly remember the first painting she shared with us, "The Romanian Blouse" by Henry Matisse. It shows a woman sitting casually, in a decorated blouse, holding a pair of beads. Her features were not clearly defined, but the artist captured the essence of the woman beautifully. I was drawn to this painting because it wasn't realistic, and it looked like Matisse colored outside of the lines. To this day, it is my favorite painting. The Picture Lady gave each of us oil pastels and a large piece of expensive paper and instructed us to create something similar in Matisse's style. I had not worked with oil pastels before, and it was as if she gave me a new language in which to communicate.

During my undergraduate classes, someone wrote on the wall of our painting studio: "Everybody is a genius. But if you judge a fish by its ability to climb a tree, it will live its whole life believing that it is stupid." From ages 11 to 21, I was a fish climbing a tree, except to Mrs. G and the Picture Lady. It wasn't until I began Art Education classes that I realized I was smart, just not in a traditional way. I loved learning about different art-making activities and ways to motivate students to be their best creative selves. Student teaching was a complete joy. Teaching came easy to me, and I felt that maybe there was a place for me in school after all.

It pains me to think about all the people in the world who feel like they are fish climbing trees. Society carves out intelligence into standardized tests and ACT scores. I am not dismissing this form of aptitude, I believe in a broader spectrum of smarts, not a "one style fits all" system of education.

Dr. Howard Gardner, professor of education at Harvard University, identifies eight categories of intelligence in his Theory of Multiple Intelligences: verbal-linguistic, logical-mathematical, visual-spatial, bodily-kinesthetic, musical-rhythmic, interpersonal, intrapersonal, and naturalistic. We are all familiar with the "dumb jock" stereotype. Under Gardner's theory, the jock is considered a bodily-kinesthetic intelligent athlete.

When we spend our lives comparing ourselves to the "smart kids in class," we overlook our natural gifts and talents. Many young people fall between the cracks at school because their form of intelligence is overlooked and misunderstood. Unfortunately, in my experience working with youth, most students who drop out of high school and either land in the criminal justice system or earn minimum wage and spend their lives below the poverty line fall into this category. This is a critical concern because it shapes generations of families. As adults, we must change our vision of intelligence and invest in our youth. I am not sure where I would be without loving parents, Mrs. G, and the Picture Lady.

History is filled with misfits who managed to rise above difficulty and succeed despite their limitations. Steve Jobs was a college dropout, and reportedly collected Coke® bottles for money. Elon Musk was so introspective as a child, his parents thought he might be deaf. Until he was 15, Musk was severely bullied. Joan of Arc, a peasant girl living in medieval times, lead France to victory in its long-running war with England.

Many of my much-loved misfits are found in the Bible. God entrusted Moses, despite his speech impediment, with the Ten Commandments and ordered him to lead the Jewish people out of slavery. Jesus, my favorite misfit, was considered a radical for going against the teachings of the high priests and Pharisees. Jesus befriended the lepers, tax collectors, and prostitutes. His willingness to go against social convention and embrace all of humanity has shaped me to the core.

Society does not always celebrate creative souls and unconventional thinkers. Perhaps, it is because we fear what we do not understand. Maybe it feels safer to put people in boxes. Whatever the case, I am inspired by the misfits who went before me. Their stories of perseverance give me hope. Let us encourage one another to find our genius. It is time to liberate the many fish out there trying to climb trees.

TOO TALL TO BE AN ASTRONAUT: REVISIONING CHILDHOOD DREAMS

At one point or another we've all been asked, "What do you want to be when you grow up?" The usual responses are doctor, artist, rock star, professional athlete, policeman, President of the United States, etc. When we are young, we dream boldly and without fear or limitation. The future is filled with possibility and wonder.

In the third grade, I told Mrs. Truman I wanted to be an astronaut. She chuckled a little and explained, "Honey, you're too tall to be an astronaut." This saddened me on a deep level, but I believed her. After, all she was the teacher. I had no choice but to redirect my dreams to fit a tall person's job. In the sixth grade, I decided to be a firefighter. I liked the idea of carrying people out of burning buildings and climbing ladders to rescue scared cats from trees. However, Father McClean said I would never be able to lift as much as a man, and I would not be permitted to fight fires. I stopped telling adults what I wanted to be when I grew up.

In high school, I shared with Sister Benedicta, my favorite teacher, that I was thinking about becoming a Sister of Charity. I was drawn to teaching and loved God.

"Sarah, you like beer and boys too much to become a nun," she lovingly told me. Her feedback didn't hurt me because deep down, I knew she was correct. She saw the real me. I eventually made it through undergraduate school and held on to my dream of being an art teacher. As an educator, I recognized the giant responsibility I inherited. Students were impressionable and fragile, just as I was at their age. They had dreams, high hopes, and goals beyond measure. I did my best to keep young children's dreams alive no matter how tall, short, or physically capable the students were. I wished Mrs. Truman and Father McClean would have done this for me.

Teaching art was a complete joy. I designed assignments big enough for students to imagine their future within the context of their dreams. I extended their projects further by asking a big "WHY?" behind their dream. When a young boy said he wanted to be a famous athlete, I asked why, and he replied, "Because I would be rich, and I could buy my momma a house."

A young girl wanted to be the president and explained, "I would make laws so that no one was allowed to live in a house with cock-roaches and bedbugs."

Another girl dreamt of becoming a doctor so she could find a cure for diabetes. There were always a few children who wanted riches and fame for their own sake, but most of my students had a reason behind their dreams.

Life moves fast. One minute you're sitting at your school desk making plans to run for the president of the United States, and the next minute you turn into an accountant or a plumber. Both are noble professions, just not ones I have heard from the mouths of children. So, what happens to our lost childhood dreams? Do they get tucked away for the next generation? Do they get buried under dirty laundry? Are they still a part of us?

If we can go back to our younger selves and ask the big "WHY?," we might find that our dreams haven't been lost at all. Many of us are living our dream; it's just not obvious. I never made it as an astronaut, I still admire the stars. On difficult days, I close my eyes and imagine sitting on the moon, viewing the earth from more than 200,000 miles away. I am not a firefighter, but I like to think I help rescue the people I serve. Perhaps not from flames, but addiction, lack of hope, and despair. And Sister Benedicta was right, I am happily married and a recovering alcoholic. I love God even more than I did in high school, and I do my best to glorify Him in my daily life.

Our jobs might not be as sensational as our younger selves would have wanted, but where would we be without plumbers, sanitation workers, or bricklayers? The value we place on our life should not come from a job title but rather how we live our life. Instead of asking children "what" they want to be when they grow up, the real question could be "who" do they want to become when they grow up.

God gave each of us a role to play on earth; not a small role, but a giant and noble one. Mother Teresa once said, "If you want to change the world, go home and love your family."

We are called to love one another; we are called to be of service; we are called to ease the suffering around us. If ever you find yourself disappointed by where life has taken you — look around, with wide-open eyes, and see where your love is needed.

GULF SHRIMP CANTONESE: WE BELONG TO EACH OTHER

We celebrated my mother-in-law's 85th birthday at a lovely restaurant. After dinner, I took a cell-phone call outside. It was a rainy night, and many guests were huddled under the canopy waiting for the valet to return with their cars. I noticed a familiar young woman dressed in medical scrubs sitting on the steps with a faraway look in her eye. I made eye contact with her while I was on the phone and offered her a smile. She didn't smile back. As I hung up the phone and began to walk up the stairs, I heard a voice from behind me say,

"Hey! Wait a minute, I think we painted a dove together at the hospital."

"Of course! How are you?"

"I'm waiting for my friend to get off work. I have nine months left at medical-assisting school. What do you think of that?"

"I think that's great. You are making things happen in your life."

"Really? You think that's great?"

"Yes, I am proud of you. Are you hungry?" I asked, remembering she was a psychiatric patient I served. She indicated that she was hungry and I invited her into the restaurant.

We walked up the steps to the bar and found a seat for her. I told the bartender that I would like to buy my friend's dinner and asked if we could see some menus. He brought out an appetizer menu and the main course menu. She sheepishly looked at the appetizer menu.

"Their specialty is ribs. Do you like ribs?"

She told me she liked shrimp. I took the main course menu sitting in front of her, scrolled down, and showed her the Gulf Shrimp Cantonese.

"That costs $22.99!" she exclaimed with big eyes.

"Yes, I know, and you're worth it."

She smiled for the first time that night as tears fell from her face. I imagined her tears expressed many things. Perhaps it was being told she was worthy of an expensive meal, or that I was proud of the steps she was taking to regain her life.

I ordered her dinner and paid the bill. I apologized that I couldn't stay because my family was on their way out.

She offered to get her meal to go, rather than eat at the bar, and explained her friend wouldn't be off work for two-and-a-half hours.

"I don't belong here. I can eat it on the steps where I saw you before." Her words stopped me in my tracks. I sensed her desire to be invisible.

"You belong here, just as anyone else does. I hope you will sit here away from the rain. Watch TV and enjoy your dinner."

The bartender picked up on the situation, came over, offered her a smile, and said, "Stay here, ma'am. We are happy to have you."

She seemed satisfied, and I stood up to leave. She jumped off the barstool, hugged me, and whispered, "I still have that dove painting we worked on together. I am staying at the shelter, but when I get my own place, it will be the first thing I put on the wall." She thanked me for dinner, and I walked downstairs to meet my family.

The woman's words, *I don't belong here*, stuck in my heart. It was as if I could feel the heaviness of her life, the rejection, and her quiet suffering. I thought about the many people I serve who live in the margins. The margins are dark and lonely places; they can strip people of their dignity and identity. I wondered how many people experience the feeling of not belonging each day. I thought of my own life and times when I felt I did not belong.

I am fortunate to say that it has been a long time since I felt I did not belong. I attribute this perspective to my renewed understanding of God's love for us: God loves all His children equally. We are all family, brothers, and sisters bonded together by humanity.

Mother Teresa said, "If we have no peace, it is because we have forgotten that we belong to each other." This beautiful truth is easy to forget. The woman in scrubs is my sister, and I had a responsibility to see that she did not go hungry or feel unwanted. I had a responsibility to remind her that she was loved, that she belonged. My encounter with this woman brought me great joy. I believe pieces of me that felt inadequate and unworthy were mended by showing compassion toward this woman.

I prayed for people everywhere who felt unwanted, invisible, and unworthy of belonging. I prayed that God would release His angels on earth to seek out the lonely and wrap them in blankets of love. As I drove home, I imagined that woman, sitting in her scrubs, eating

Gulf Shrimp Cantonese at the bar, and watching recaps of the US women's soccer team's victory on the television.

GRAFFITI ON THE DOOR: TEACHABLE MOMENTS

I was 22 years old when I accepted my first job teaching art at an urban high school. I was eager to save the world, as are many young adults. I spent weeks during the summer preparing my classroom for the year ahead. I painted the dingy cinderblock walls a cheerful yellow. I carefully cut out giant letters that spelled "KNOWLEDGE IS POWER" and taped them to the front wall. I searched the building for available tables and chairs and lugged them to my classroom located on the second floor. I cleaned out closets and salvaged any paint and brushes that survived the previous year. Lastly, I placed real plants along the window ledge. I was proud of the room transformation and ready to begin inspiring the next generation.

I remember clearly my drive to school on the first day. I spent time thanking God for the job as many of my peers had not yet found work. I prayed that I would inspire my students to be the best versions of themselves. I hummed along with Crosby, Stills, Nash & Young singing "Teach Your Children." I arrived 30 minutes early. As I approached my class, I was assaulted by the words "WHITE BITCH" spray-painted across my door. I stood frozen as reality settled in. Clearly, there was a history there I was not aware of: a history of mistrust and assumptions.

Thirty minutes later, the first bell rang. I desperately wanted to address my students with something real and meaningful. I wanted to move past this huge issue of race quickly and with purpose. I sat alone in my big and empty classroom. Students were beginning to arrive, and I heard lockers click open and shut. I looked around the room, hoping an answer would fall from the ceiling. The clock was ticking. Before I knew it, students filled the room. The bell rang, and I still had no words.

I cleared my throat and declared with an authoritative voice, "Welcome to art class. I am your teacher. Although we don't know each other, you may have an idea of who I am, and I may have an idea of who you are. Our ideas may be right, and they may be wrong. Let's give it some time before we make up our minds." I believe my students were listening to me because they appeared confused.

"Why are you saying this to us?" one boy asked.

"I want us to give each other a chance. We need to start the year fresh. Some of you may get into a lot of trouble; I don't know who you are. Others of you are A students, but I don't know you either. At this moment, we are all on good terms with each other. I hope we can keep it this way." The class seemed satisfied, and I began teaching.

I don't think I ever worked as hard in my life as I did during that first year of teaching. I memorized the names of all 300 students, fought administration for money to buy quality supplies, and arranged a field trip to the art museum. I also started an art club. I called parents and complimented their children. But perhaps most importantly, I kept my initial promise of keeping an open mind toward my students. It worked. Many of my colleagues were astonished by my rapport with the "troublemakers." They asked how I motivated my students to behave and produce work, but I didn't have an answer at the time. However, it's evident to me now: I used the graffiti to motivate me to establish deeper relationships with my students. I had a choice when I saw the spray paint on my door. I could have started the year off reprimanding students, or I could have used it as a teachable moment. I chose the second, and it made all the difference.

When tensions or difficulty arise, there is always an opportunity to gain insight. We must find the teachable moment, the real-world opportunity to learn from the present situation. These moments are unplanned and fleeting. First, you must recognize the conflict. Then consider the perspectives of all parties involved. Lastly, frame the moment in commonality. Seize the opportunity when it arrives. You may feel vulnerable and clumsy; that's okay. Find the humanity in the situation and pray to God for guidance. It has worked well for me over the years.

Anyone who desires to change the world will face similar obstacles. Your graffiti may look different than mine. You might be facing cynicism, arrogance, or ignorance. Whatever your graffiti is, allow it to motivate your efforts, but not detour them. Search for the teachable moment, and you will gain insight into the larger picture. Allow your graffiti to broaden your perspective so you may have a better understanding of the issue at hand and the people it affects.

Whatever your graffiti is, allow it to motivate your efforts, but not detour them.

I think I learned more than my students did during that year, as I discovered mistrust and assumptions take a long time to repair. I also realized that so much is possible with a consistent and sustained effort. I recognized conflict doesn't have to hurt if we can channel it into dialogue and action. Tensions can be a catalyst for authentic transformation. I am grateful for that graffiti and the lessons it taught me. Long after "White Bitch" was removed from my door, someone wrote in black permanent marker, "Miss B. the art teacher." I remain very proud of that title.

SWIMMING WITH ROYALTY: UNIVERSAL BELONGING

In my mid-20s, I accepted a teaching position for a Department of Defense School located in the Middle Eastern nation of Bahrain. I taught art to American military children in kindergarten through 12th grade and to the country's wealth and royalty. I also coached the school's swim program and privately taught the young son of a royal family. I never spoke directly to the parents of the young boy; a staff member of the family made all the arrangements. A few days before our first lesson, a man called for my address so their driver could pick me up and take me to a luxury hotel, where I would coach the boy.

At exactly 4:30 p.m. on the appointed day, a shiny behemoth SUV pulled up in front of my compound. The windows were darkly tinted, and I was not able to see who was inside the vehicle. I walked cautiously toward the car, where a man rolled down the window, and through broken English asked if I was the coach. I nodded yes, and he motioned for me to get in the car. A seven-year-old boy sat on the first row of seats. Sitting in the row behind him were three women dressed head to toe in abayas, long black cloaks that wrapped around the head and body. The women were also wearing black gloves and their faces were covered except for their eyes. I nervously and enthusiastically greeted everyone. No one acknowledged me, and I took a seat next to the boy.

We drove in silence to the hotel for what seemed like an eternity. We finally made it to the entrance. Palm trees lined the street, and real grass grew on the ground. I hadn't seen grass in a long time, and it made me think of home back in Ohio. The driver pulled up to the main entrance, where two uniformed hotel employees were waiting for our arrival. I was the first to get out of the car, followed by the boy, and then the three women. The employees' English was limited, but they were aware of our coming to use the indoor pool. The pool was breathtaking with large windows on the ceiling, walls lined with Moroccan tile, and giant flower arrangements placed intermittently within the space. One of the hotel employees asked if I needed to change clothes. I shook my head no; I was wearing my bathing suit under my clothes. One of the women took the boy to a changing room.

The boy returned, and the three women took a seat alongside the pool. I began to undress and felt the women's eyes looking at me. I was in my bathing suit, half naked, while they were covered in all black except for their eyes and toes. At that moment, I felt exposed but not necessarily embarrassed. I smiled at the boy and instructed him to get in the water after me. Our first lesson would be floating on our backs. I demonstrated and held my hand under his back as he attempted to float. His nervousness and tenseness made floating very difficult. We moved on to simple bobs hoping he would get more comfortable in the water.

As we bobbed in and out of the water, I saw his fears subside. He looked at me as if he was asking permission to have fun, and I smiled back at him. He laughed, and we took turns splashing each other. I asked him if we could try floating on our backs again, and he agreed.

This time, I moved my body underwater so the boy could rest his head on my shoulder as he floated, which was much more successful. I was reminded of the universal truth that when we support and raise each other, life is easier for everyone.

As the boy's head rested on my shoulder, I looked at the women, all dressed in black sitting next to us. I badly wanted to see their facial expressions. I struggled with how the women dressed. I wasn't sure if it was a religious symbol or a form of oppression. I wondered how they saw me. Did they want to be swimming or were they happy watching? Did they resent me as a Westerner in a bathing suit, or could they envision themselves in the water? I will never know for certain, but I wanted them to be happy. I felt blessed to be an American woman. I am fully aware of the progress that still needs to be made in the United States, but I was just so grateful to be in that bathing suit and not sitting next to the pool.

Our lesson came to an end, and the women caretakers spoke to the boy in Arabic. He obediently got out of the pool, and one woman took him to the changing room. When they returned, the boy was smiling from ear to ear. I like to think the caretaker praised him. The driver was waiting outside for us. We assumed our previous positions in the car. The driver asked how the boy did, and I assured everyone he was very brave. I saw the man smile for the first time in the rear-view mirror. As we drove away, two of the women handed fresh-squeezed orange juice and sugar cookies to the boy and me. I smiled and said, "Shukran," which means "thank you." The women's eyes seemed softer as if they were smiling back at me.

The boy and I continued swim lessons for a year with much of the same routine. I grew to love the fresh-squeezed orange juice and sugar cookies on our rides home. They somehow represented a feeling of belonging. Despite our social, religious, and ethnic differences, we were very much the same. We all wanted that boy to swim;

we all had something to share. I have learned through many different cultural experiences that we can experience this sense of belonging if we take a step outside of our comfort zone and trust in the goodness of the human connection.

A BAG OF FUNYUNS: GENEROSITY OF SPIRIT

I have been painting with women at our city's largest homeless shelter for years. Many of the women are affected by trauma, mental illness, and addiction. Their lives are in a state of transition, and they are always happy to see me show up with my bag of watercolor paints. We listen to music, paint, pray, laugh, and cry. I have grown to cherish our time together. The women generously share with me their stories, their talents, and their tears. Although we all come from diverse paths, our differences quickly fade as we come together to engage in the art-making process with an open heart and mind.

I have met hundreds, maybe thousands, of women, but Chantelle stands out as one of the most memorable. For three months, every Wednesday, she showed up like clockwork. Her routine rarely changed. Each week she sat down, offered a huge smile, thanked us for being there, and then she would dig into her gigantic purse and offer me a bag of Funyuns. After I accepted the fried onion snack, she would ask me to play Earth, Wind & Fire's, "Let's Groove." She would close her eyes, sway in her chair, and sing every word ... loudly and in key. She always appeared jovial and lighthearted, as if she didn't have a single care in the world.

One summer night, only a few women showed up for painting, and we decided to move class outside. The group was happy to get out of the frigid air conditioning and into the late summer air. Chantelle was particularly thrilled to work outside. I don't meet many people in her circumstance that spread joy as freely and frequently as she did, and I wanted to learn more about her. I asked her to share her story with me, and she happily agreed. In a steady voice, Chantelle told me that her 15-year-old son was recently murdered by gunshot and, three weeks later, her house burned to the ground. Her words were sobering and caught me off guard. I never expected to hear the extent of her loss and the pain that she endured. Her attitude and behavior told a much different story.

Toward the end of our conversation, the sun was beginning to set. Chantelle seemed to glow. I asked her how she managed to stay so positive in the face of adversity.

She shut her eyes and asked, "Do you feel it?"

I was confused.

"Do you feel the breeze on your face? Do you see the pink in the sky? Do you hear the birds chirping?"

I nodded, yes.

"There is still so much to be thankful for. There is still so much beauty to those who choose to see it."

Chantelle's words deeply moved me.

There is still so much beauty to those who choose to see it.
Chantelle's sentiment was profound yet simple. Yes, there is so much

beauty for those who CHOOSE to see it. Her way of being in the world was a choice. She lived with intention, purpose, and clarity. Never once did she play the role of victim. She was the master of her thoughts; she was the captain of her life. I was reminded of Proverbs 31:25 (NIV), "She is clothed with strength and dignity; she can laugh at the days to come." Although her only possessions were a suitcase full of clothes, she was the richest and most generous person I knew.

Chantelle was generous in sharing her pain with me, but perhaps even more importantly, she was generous with sharing her joy. Her joy lifted the entire shelter. Despite her horrific life circumstances, she somehow was able to not only survive but thrive in spirit. She was always present, sang unapologetically, and joyfully created art. She was the first to congratulate another woman who found housing. Chantelle personified what I call "generosity of spirit."

Chantelle was generous in spirit because she gave of herself so willingly to others; she was kind and joyful despite her pain and struggle. She took complete responsibility for her emotions and encouraged others to do the same. Chantelle was grateful for the small things and found miracles all around her. Generosity of spirit requires us to rise above the struggle and to see the good in ourselves, others, and the world. We can decide each day how we will orient ourselves in this world. We can view the world through the eyes of a cynic and see corruption and deceit, or we can choose to be generous in spirit and view the world through possibility, potential, and wonder.

Generosity of spirit requires us to rise above the struggle and to see the good in ourselves, others, and the world.

I believe we are all capable of being like Chantelle. Generosity of spirit begins on a soul level. It is an offering of oneself to others. It is vulnerable, and it understands the human condition. Every time we are generous in spirit, we free ourselves and others from the shackles of despair. Chantelle has become a hero of mine. I will never look at a bag of Funyuns without thinking of Chantelle and hearing "Let's Groove." I will take time to feel the breeze on my face, see the color in the skies, and listen to the sweet melodies of the birds.

STANDING IN THE RAIN: FINDING JOY IN THE STRUGGLE

If we are not careful, life can beat the joy out of us. Many people work jobs that make them miserable. Parents are tired from raising children or being caregivers to elderly family members. There is always a chore unfinished at home. Money is often tight. The news reports the ugly in the world, with little emphasis on the good. Each day presents new challenges. The bottom line is — joy is a brave decision on how you will respond to life.

One night, after we enjoyed a dinner at a fancy restaurant, I was waiting in the rain for my husband to get the car. A man in shabby clothes and crazy hair approached me. In the back of my mind, I assumed he would ask me for money.

"Hey, lady what are you doing?" I told him I was waiting for my husband to get the car.

"No, lady, what are you doing in the rain without an umbrella?" He handed his pink polka-dotted broken umbrella to me and stood in the rain uncovered. His gesture moved me. I observed a luminous joy about him as the rain fell on his face. I invited him to share the umbrella and we talked. I learned he was a homeless veteran and a recovering addict, 90 days clean and sober.

I congratulated him on his victory and asked how he stayed so happy despite the obstacle of being homeless.

"Because ma'am, 91 days ago, I would have begged you for money to buy crack cocaine. Today, I am sober and standing under an umbrella with a classy lady," he replied.

My husband pulled up, and I asked the man where he would spend the night. He told me not to worry, God would provide for him just like he has for the past 90 days. I shook his hand good-bye and whispered, "Amen."

I am so glad to have spent time in the rain with that man. He shared one of his only possessions, a broken umbrella, but more importantly, he shared his joy. He chose to respond to his life, no matter how big the hardships, with gratitude and joy in his heart. As I drove home that night, I noticed that I was happier. It was as if he rekindled something inside me. His joy was contagious.

Once a week, I paint with Cindy, who was born with the disease of Mitochondrial Myopathy. She is confined to a wheelchair and has limited use of her hands. Her parents disowned her due to a religious belief system that does not allow medical care and now she lives in poverty. Cindy is a deeply spiritual woman and rich in her relationship with God. She LOVES to make art. We spend early Monday afternoons painting and listening to music. One of her favorite songs is "You Say" by Lauren Daigle.

Although Cindy had difficulty speaking, she would do her best to sing, especially to the verse:

You say I am loved when I can't feel a thing
You say I am strong when I think I am weak
You say I am held when I am falling short
When I don't belong, oh You say that I am Yours.

One Monday, while listening to Cindy sing, I noticed her bravery. Although she was slowly losing her ability to talk, she sang as the lyrics would overwhelm her to tears. I asked if they were sad tears.

"Were you listening to the lyrics, Sarah? They are happy tears because I am so very loved." Her response humbled me.

Cindy asked me if it was possible for her to volunteer with my ministry. I wanted to include her in any way I could, but I knew it would be a challenge to find a location that she could easily navigate in her large electric wheelchair. We decided she would write "Hope Notes" to be delivered to the homeless downtown. My friend Barb designed this concept. On one side of a blank card Cindy made art and on the other side of the card she composed a message to be received by someone experiencing difficulty. I watched Cindy struggle to write as she worked. It was time for me to leave, and I kissed her on her head. When I came back the following week, Cindy had a Hope Note finished. On one side, she painted "The Good Shepard," and on the other side in big wobbly letters, she wrote, "God loves you." The joy Cindy found in making art, and her unshakeable faith, inspired me.

I imagine many people looking in from the outside would think Cindy and the man with the umbrella have few reasons to be joyful. Often, we must experience things we don't understand. We are not guaranteed days without struggle. When trials of any kind happen, we have choices. We can be angry at God and turn away from Him, or we can run toward Him. No matter how difficult your life may seem, always remember, joy runs deeper than despair. Consider this perspective, "Nothing happens to you, it happens for you." Sometimes God protects us from what we think we want and later blesses us with what our soul needs. Struggles are meant to cleanse us and shape us into better versions of ourselves. Character cannot develop in easy times, only through struggle do we know what we are made of. Allow your broken dreams to become blessed things and find joy in the struggle.

Allow your broken dreams to become blessed things and find joy in the struggle.

DAD'S FOUR RULES: WHAT GOVERNS YOUR LIFE?

I am blessed to have been raised by two loving parents. My dad is an automobile mechanic, and my mom stayed at home while my siblings and I were in school. We ate dinner as a family every night at 6:00. Each night at dinner, our parents asked us about our day, and at least once a week, my father went over his four rules for life. They seemed simple at the time, but now as an adult, I see they were rather genius. His rules were, and still are:

1. Be yourself.

2. Stay out of jail.

3. Get to Heaven.

4. Help someone along the way.

Here is my adult interpretation of my dad's four rules:

1. BE YOURSELF.

Outside of teaching me to have faith in a loving God, this is the best gift my father gave me. The relationship we have with ourselves sets the tone for all the other relationships we have in our life. I was six feet tall in the eighth grade. At a time in most of our lives where we want to blend in, I stood a full head over my classmates and most teachers. You can imagine my peers poked fun at me and nicknamed me the Jolly Green Giant. It upset me, and I shared it with my family around the dinner table. My parents and siblings encouraged me to laugh with the crowd. If they couldn't upset me, they would stop. And they were right. I left grade school and was no longer called the Jolly Green Giant, except once.

During my freshman year in high school, I decided to embrace my inner Jolly Green Giant and dressed up as him for Halloween. My cousin Kati, who is about five feet tall, dressed as Little Green Sprout. We took the Metro bus home from school that day.

As we boarded the bus, a high school boy pointed at me and said, "Who are you supposed to be?! The Jolly Green Giant!"

I held my head high, smiled, and said, "Yes. Yes, I am the Jolly Green Giant."

My dad's first rule gave me permission to feel safe in my own skin, to feel that I am enough.

It was liberating. My dad's first rule gave me permission to feel safe in my own skin, to feel that I am enough. I was taught that I do not need to change so people will like me. If I remain myself, the right people will come into my life, and I will know love. There is a true freedom that comes into our life when we decide to embrace who we are as an individual.

2. STAY OUT OF JAIL.

This rule seemed simple as a child when I thought only bank robbers went to jail. After knowing hundreds of inmates and their stories, I recognize good people with trauma often turn to drugs and alcohol to dull their pain and too frequently wind up in jail.

3. GET TO HEAVEN

This rule also seemed obvious to me. As a child, I couldn't wait to get to Heaven. When our priest described Heaven, I imagined the small field close to our house. During the spring, it was filled with dandelions that seemed to go on forever. Heaven was explained as a place of pure love, where we feel no pain, and where we get to be reunited with the ones we have loved and lost. I remember sitting in the church pew as a child and dreaming about seeing the grandfather that I have never met. I have seen pictures of him sitting in his wheel-chair. I imagined my grandfather in Heaven, able to stand tall to greet me, in a patchwork field of dandelions.

As an adult, I view Heaven in a similar way. However, I now see the path to Heaven as a bit narrower than I did as a child. Music tells us there is a highway to Hell and only a stairway to Heaven. The highway to Hell is larger and easier to travel, but it's a selfish route. The stairway to Heaven requires discipline and sacrifice. I believe we get to Heaven by living an intentional life and being of service to the world. We get to Heaven by practicing good deeds and bringing others closer to their God.

4. HELP SOMEONE ALONG THE WAY

My parents instilled within me at a very early age, the importance of helping others. I frequently accompanied my mother to the soup kitchen. I watched her serve food to a group of diverse and hungry people. My father gave change to people on street corners and taught us the importance of being nonjudgmental. He reminded us that it is impossible to know someone's full story just by their appearance.

My ministry work takes me to the streets of my city. Through years of experience, I can spot a person who needs a meal, drug rehabilitation, or who just needs to be seen. One day I met a woman wearing flip-flops that were taped on the bottom. I had time on my hands and offered to take her to buy a new pair of shoes. She got in my car with suspicion and she asked why I was doing this for her. I told her God had told me to. This satisfied her, and she asked if we could turn up the music, her favorite song "Sweet Caroline" was playing.

I can't help but feel in life that we are all just walking each other home. By home, I mean Heaven. I love the fourth rule. It makes the world feel smaller, and it gives us a clear purpose on earth. This rule allows us to live with intention and makes life worth living.

I am grateful to my parents, who sacrificed so much for our family. I am grateful for all the meals my mother cooked, for the opportunity to help people on their walk home, and to have my father's rules to live by. I believe that, in order to have a healthy perspective, we need to establish rules to live by. We must identify the core values we hold. Our value system should be shaped by a universal standard of goodness and virtue. Our rules should govern our perspective. What are the values you hold and the rules you live by?

A LAST WISH:
GOODNESS FROM WITHIN

I received a call from a Catholic sister asking me to visit a woman in hospice. The only information she provided me was that her name was Sherri, she wanted to paint, and she had one to three weeks to live. I arranged a visit for the following day. This was not the first time I worked with a person who was actively dying. I always consider it a high honor to love someone in their final days. I also believe that time shared with the dying is a sacred one. I knew from experience that the space between me and Sherri would be an honest one with no room for pretense, small talk, or excuses.

As I drove to the hospice center, I prayed to God that He would put the right words in my heart and on my lips. In my head, I rehearsed how I would introduce myself, what I would say, and the music I could play for Sherri. My wish was to bring her peace. I was intrigued by her desire to paint and wondered what she wanted to express during the final days of her life.

I arrived at the hospice center and was instructed to put on a gown, mask, and gloves before entering the room. Once dressed, I looked at my reflection in the window and noticed that only my eyes were visible. As I entered the room, I saw a pale, beautiful young woman sleeping peacefully in the bed. I stood looking at her and thought of how pure and serene she looked. I took a seat in the chair next to her bed, wishing I could take off all my protective garb and look more human.

As Sherri slowly opened her eyes, I greeted her.

"Hi Sherri, I am Sarah. I am told you would like to do some painting."

She smiled at me and said, "I know who you are Miss Sarah. We painted together in the jail. I asked for you to visit me."

"Of Course! So good to see you." The truth is that I meet hundreds of people in my ministry work and it is next to impossible to remember every face and every name. However, in that moment she embodied all the brokenhearted people I have worked with. I felt an urgency and a strong desire to help her in any way possible.

I cleared off her bedside table and arranged watercolor paints and paper. I played music, and we began to paint. I watched as she painted and I saw the child she once was.

After painting for 20, minutes or so she said to me, "Miss Sarah do you think I can go with you the next time you go to the jail to paint?" Her request caught me off guard.

"I am not sure how your doctors would feel about you being exposed to all those germs."

"Don't you think I should be able to decide how I want to spend my last days on earth?"

I met Sherri's gaze and with a lump in my throat. "Yes, I agree. But I am curious why you want to go to the jail with me? You have a beautiful room here, giant television, and warm meals."

"Because I want to be a part of the peace you bring the women."

I like to think that at that moment, Sherri represented the best in all of us. Her dying wish wasn't to see the ocean or meet a celebrity. Her dying wish was to bring peace to someone else. I like to believe that at our core, all humans share her desire to be of service to others. We must, as a country, as a world, get back to our core goodness. Unfortunately, society pushes many distractions into the people we were designed to be. The news fills us with fear, and social media tells us we are not enough. The truth is we were born enough. Sherri, on her death bed, stripped of her health and all worldly possessions was so much more than enough. Her desire to help alleviate suffering made her noble in my eyes.

In time, I learned more about Sherri's life. Her life wasn't easy. As a young girl she was diagnosed with a serious chronic illness. She endured sexual abuse as a child and later turned to drugs to alleviate her pain. As an adult she entered prostitution to support her drug habit.

I will forever cherish my time with Sherri. We talked about God's love and I shared with her my perceptions of Heaven. I repeatedly played the Catholic hymn "Be Not Afraid," for her. Together we sang the chorus,

Be not afraid
I go before you always.

Come, follow me,
And I will give you rest.

As doctors predicted, Sherri died two weeks after we met. Her life ended close to the 4th of July. I couldn't help but think how appropriate it was that she passed away so close to the day when we celebrate freedom. At last, Sherri was free. She was free from illness, addiction, and trauma. Her last wish had a profound impact on me. It reinforced my belief that at our core, we are generous and loving people. I carry Sherri's legacy with me, and it informs my practice. We never made it to the jail together, but her spirit lives on through my work.

THE STARS IN THE SKY: A PERSPECTIVE ON DEATH AND DYING

If there is one thing that doesn't discriminate, it is that all humans age; all humans will die. There is simply no escaping it. Eventually, our bodies will stop working, and our heart will stop beating. I find myself getting older — wanting to age gracefully, with purpose, and without regret.

Through providence, I found a wonderful mentor in Sister Grace. She was a Franciscan Sister of the Poor. Sister operated a day center for women in trafficking and sexual exploitation. She possessed a deep, unconditional, and maternal love for the women on the street, and they, in turn, loved her like a mother. The way Sister interacted with the marginalized was inspiring. She met everyone with compassion, grace, and zero judgment.

Although there were 40 years between us, we became quick friends. Sister Grace was eccentric. She loved to dye her hair red and mix Sweet'N Low into her wine. She was quick to laugh. Years into our

relationship, Sister grew ill. I sat next to her when she was diagnosed with stage four cancer. She was saddened by the news, but not
hysterical in any way. Few words were spoken on our ride home from
the hospital.

"Can I spend the night at your house?" she quietly asked.

"For as long as you want." She spent some of her final weeks
on my couch.

My memories of those days are precious to me. We would watch the
popular television show *The Bachelor* and take bets on which woman
the handsome star would choose. She and my husband watched
old movies including *Rear Window, The Bellboy,* and *The Flim-Flam
Man.* After chemotherapy, the only meals she managed to eat were
Egg McMuffins from McDonald's. There were several left over in our
freezer from the many people who visited her.

Sister Grace and I had countless and intimate conversations about
her past, her desire to serve God, and her vision of Heaven. She
entered the convent at a very early age knowing she was born to be
of service. Sister explained how she saw the face of Christ in those
she ministered. She believed with all her being that she would be
reunited with her loved ones in Heaven. My relationship with Sister
Grace reminds me of the poem, "The Old Astronomer to His Pupil"
written in 1868 by Sarah Williams.

Williams wrote this poem both retrospectively and with a vision of
a future beyond death. She wrote within the context of a relationship
between teacher and pupil. Many believe the narrator was intended
to be the voice of Galileo, communicating to his pupil on issues such
as maturing, old age, and the sentiments he felt toward death. Below
is my favorite vignette:

"Though my soul may set in darkness, it will rise in perfect light;

I have loved the stars too fondly to be fearful of the night."

Sister Grace was my Galileo. She taught me how to live, and she taught me how to die. She was a fearless woman. I witnessed this through her interactions with the men and women on the city streets. I saw it when she received the news of her terminal illness. I felt it in the laughter we shared during her final days. She loved so boldly that it made her unafraid of her own death. I imagine all the stars in the sky to be the lives that Sister touched. I knew our loving Father was guiding her among the stars and into His arms. I knew she rose in perfect light. With this perspective, the stars don't feel so far away and neither do the ones we love.

ACKNOWLEDGMENTS

I am so very blessed to live a storied life filled with beautiful people. In thinking about what and who made this book possible, by sincere gratitude belongs to the following:

My God, who guides me through it all.

Brian, my devoted husband, with whom I become more myself each day.

Judy and Tom Bonhaus — my parents, and first teachers on love and life.

Tom, Matt and Maria (Sissy) — my siblings. Because of you, I will never be alone in this world.

Ruth Hellmann, for all her love and the delicious meals she cooks for me.

Barb BOO BOO Griffin, my cheerleader, a true friend and inspiration.

Dr. Angela Arndt, my comrade.

Dana, wise beyond her years.

Wanda, a beautiful soul if I ever met one.

Kati, my cousin, life-long friend and companion.

Dr. Miriam Raidor-Roth, advisor and friend.

Sister Benedicta, Diane Gallagher, Mary Ann Deak (the picture Lady)
— true educators.

Cathy Fyock, writing mentor.

My editorial board, Patrice Eby Burke, Kim Bill and Rachel Short. This
book is stronger because of you.

The Delta Gams, with whom I would go to war.

My Seton High School friends, for the history we share.

Kate Colbert and the entire team at Silver Tree Publishing.

Lastly, to the beautiful souls I have served over the years. Because
of you, I know empathy and compassion, and have a better understanding of myself.

ABOUT THE AUTHOR

Dr. Sarah Hellmann is an
author, artist, and speaker.
After receiving her PhD
in Education from the
University of Cincinnati, she
founded the ministry Art for
All People, inspired by her
own struggles with mental

illness and addiction. Sarah believes that when dealing with pain,
addiction, and loss, there are often no words to explain the extent of
suffering. This is when the language of the arts becomes essential.
Her mission is to inspire others to use their inherent creativity toward
healing and empowerment.

Sarah believes that there is more in life that unites us rather
than divides us. This belief is the organizing principle behind
Broken-Down Jalopies and Other Short Stories. Sarah uses the power
of storytelling to illustrate the resilience and tenacity of the human
spirit. She encourages readers to live a happier and more peaceful life

by shifting their perspective to see the ordinary magic that surrounds them each day.

Sarah finds great joy through her work with inmates, veterans, survivors of trafficking, and recovering addicts. Sarah's newest endeavor is working with hospice, creating legacy art for patients near end of life. Sarah resides in Cincinnati with her husband, Brian, the love of her life and biggest fan. In her free time, Sarah can be found in her upstairs home studio or on her front porch, creating art. She is currently driving a jalopy.

ABOUT ART FOR ALL PEOPLE

The mission of Art for All People (AFAP) is to bring the arts to people who are marginalized in the community. AFAP's goal is to promote healing and reassert a sense of hope in marginalized individuals through the art-making process and trusting relationships.

AFAP is a 501(c)(3) nonprofit organization that serves people affected by human trafficking, addiction, mental illness, homelessness, and veterans suffering from addiction and PTSD.

Art touches our lives in profound ways and can bring healing to those in physical, mental, or spiritual crisis. AFAP implements transformational art projects that bridge social and economic divides to make the arts accessible to all. AFAP relies heavily on private donations.

If you are interested in supporting Art for all People, please consider making a donation at ArtForAllPeople.org/Donate or, if you're in the greater Cincinnati area, booking Sarah for your corporate team-building needs. Sarah is available to engage your team, organization, or audience with storytelling and/or art-making exercises. You may contact her by email at sarah@artforallpeople.org or visit her website at www.ArtForAllPeople.org.

GO BEYOND THE BOOK

AND KEEP IN TOUCH
WITH SARAH HELLMANN

Sarah Hellmann's unique perspective and sensitivity has been shaped by her many interactions with the people she serves. She has a solid understanding of resiliency and how it applies to our daily life. She has the soul of an artist and the skillset necessary to bring out the creativity in others. Sarah has the ability to bring groups together, and to motivate audiences to gain a renewed perspective.

Sarah is available to meet your organization's needs, in the greater Cincinnati area and beyond.

Hire her to:

- Engage your team, organization, or audience with storytelling.
- Facilitate corporate teambuilding through art-making exercises.
- Direct a retreat. These events are always centered around creativity and can be spiritual in nature, based upon request.
- Deliver a keynote address. Topics range from perspective and working collaboratively, to resiliency and self-care.

These opportunities have been proven by corporations to be energizing, inspiring, and uplifting.

"I wish we could come together and paint like this every day. I forgot how it felt to be creative. Like you said, we are all born artists ... we just need to be reminded of it."

— Proctor and Gamble, Teambuilding

"Thank you for sharing your stories on resilience and how, at the core, we are resilient people. Your creative activities allowed me to look within myself to discover new ways to look at life and work struggles."

— Cincinnati Children's Hospital, Keynote

KEEP IN TOUCH!

Sarah@ArtForAllPeople.org

www.ArtForAllPeople.org

www.Facebook.com/SarahHellmannAuthor

YOU, TOO, CAN BE A SOURCE OF LIGHT

What can you *do to continue the mission set into motion by Sarah Hellmann? So many things ...*

Reach out to the brokenhearted in your family and community. Speak positive words of encouragement over them. Be a beacon of hope.

Share your story somehow and somewhere. The world needs your contribution.

Allow yourself to see the world and its people with renewed perspective.

Support Art for all People by donating on their website at www.ArtForAllPeople.org.

Pray.

Made in the USA
Monee, IL
26 April 2020